AF200642

GALOS, Z J

# KING OF ICE

## A poetic Legend

Poetry

Impressum

Bibliographical information of the German
National Library:
The German National Library indexes this publication in
The German National Bibliography;
Detailed bibliographical data may be derived from the
Interne website http://dnb.dnb.de

©2019 GALOS, Z J

Producer and publisher: BoD – Books on Demand,
Norderstedt

ISBN: 9783750428522

Zorko discovers the entrance to the magical Iceworld

# ZINA and ZORKO

From the caverns of the Ice-world's

Castles

And their extended magical gardens

Faint murmuring reverberates

A touch of a tune emerges in its full

Melodic beauty

From the strings of a solo instrument

Powerfully ending its own composed

Cadenza.

All other instruments join in

A whole orchestra of water drops

Tumbles and falls into this cavernous

Labyrinth deep down and like

A choir of the Proms

The mountain starts to sing

To the rising sun rays baton.

A powerful symphonic sound

Shakes the dreaming Iceland

Which suddenly comes alive.

Deep in the icicled ravines the daily

Traffic starts to flow to ever changing

Shapes that melt and slide and glow

Iridescent colours that seem to rise

And fall

Like veils of Salome

In this translucent world of snow

And ice.

Moved and shifted by invisible hands

A ballet of frozen dancers will come

Quickly alive

As their performance prepares

For King Noro and his Queen of Ice

Sweet Nora in a snow flake gown.

Now that the mountain wakes

Its gigantic towers of red stone

Will store the exploding energies

Of the sun for another day

Bring alive this land of glittering

Castles

A world of untold riches lays its
Portals open to the ones who can see
Its mystical splendours
Hear the heavenly music
Of its intricate clockwork play
And feel the touches of its magic
Ever changing scenes but most of all
If you are so lucky to see the majestic
King Ice and his enchanting fairy
The Queen of Ice –
Nora the Queen of all Iceland fairies.


Brandishing their neon adverts
Calling to the outside world
With their fairground blaring music
The giants wake from within their
Deep rock infested surrounds
Their limbs become alive and as
They move and rise
The mountain stretches and sighs
Absorbing warmth and losing
Its frozen stance of Ice-world nights

A conundrum of sounds fills the air

Roars of beasts and man's every day's

Tinkering and working

Will fill the green valleys and the sheer

Water trickling gorges

A sharp signal for the daily hunt

Scuttles the game across wooded hills

And magnificent outcrops.


Excitement drives the chasers on

Fear and panic for the hunted game

Spreads like wildfire across the lands

Bursts of gunshots in the distance.


Inside the big and ice-capped tower

The sounds have changed

In this tinkering and busy working

Of millions of red-hot anvils

In the Gold- and Silversmith-World

Of king Noro's riches

As myriads of tiny hammers forge

The precious metal shapes

Into leaves and plants
Men and women and deer.
And further into any shape
One couldn't possibly imagine.


To the singing of the anvils
A multi chorus of magical chords
And pure voices compliment
Their metallic rhythmic sounds
Until their daily tasks are dutifully
Performed to near perfection
All working on a most exceptional
Royal treasure chest
The redecoration of the splendid
Great Noro Hall:
A tribute to their just and most
Honoured king.
The throne chairs for the majestic
Pair.
Their crown insignia.

The most colourful gown is made

For the Queen.

Colourful sequins joined together

With golden threads

In the colours of a most magnificent

Peacock of the protected isles

Her waist-long hair interlaced with

Thousands of natural pearls


The golden shoes for the stately affair.

Their floor long royal robes with ancient

Traditional patterns

Their master weavers will dutifully

Produce

Spun from the silken threads

A team of experienced women

Will prepare

While handpicked maidens will

Need to sew the robes

To hold the gemstones

That decorate the collars

Beside the wide-flowing hems.

The most colourful gown –

A piece of couture-art has been

Made for the Queen to try on

Her waist-long hair with the

Interlaced pearls

Compliment her fairy nature.


Sleek and shapely

Queen Nora appears

With her cape of gold

Which wraps around her

In an ever-winding serpentine design.


The clock strikes twelve

And the castle opens up for audience.

The fanfares announce the arrival

Of the King and Queen

In their breathtaking regalia.


King Noro and Queen Nora

Sweep into the Great Hall of Noro

Feather light

Floating on cushions of air.

The huge crowd assembled falls to

Its knees

And hushed it'll remain

Until the Herald of King Noro

Announces to be at ease.

The King and Queen have taken

Their seats on the crimson coloured

Thrones

To conduct their regular audience

Listen to the crowds and hear

Their lively stories of loss and pain

To receive the jesters and bards

The poets and storytellers.


So many have sung before and

Praised the virtues of the King and

The beauty of his Queen

Her warm and loving smile

Which enchants everybody

In this mountain kingdom's

Hidden paradise.

But never before has a poet dared
To sing about love and passion
Like Zorko from the Storylands.


Holding his lyre on his slightly bent
Knee
He intonates his ballade
Addressing the King
Praising his wisdom and lauding
His justice.

Then he carries on with a lyric song
Intended for the Queen and when
He has sung about her love and care
For the poor and the simple folk
Her golden heart and her compassion.


Intonating his new composition
A love song about his recent loss
Beloved and dearest ZINA:

'I knew her from childhood and

Used to watch her growing-up.

She was to me like a flower in spring

Growing pure in the snow

Like a bellflower in May

The first flower to greet me with

The sweetest fragrance

In the fresh air.


She was the warm sunshine on my face

My breath of life and more.

She touched my inner soul and let

My words come out fair and clear'.

Zorko performs his ballad for King Noro and Queen Nora
in King Noro's Hall in the Ice Palace

Zorko paused and wiped a tear
Overcome with sudden emotion.
As he composed himself again
He sees that he has gained the full
Attention of the Queen –


'I often told her about my admiration
My care for her and my intentions.
She would just smile and tell me
She was made for me
She can see that it was meant to be.
But would it be wise to challenge fate
When the Gods do not protect
Perfection?
'And that's what worried her!'

Zina's Premonition

Zorko sung many songs for Zina

As they grew up to become good

Good friends.

One summer night he kissed her

And swore her eternal love.

Zina cried as she could not help

Herself

To be overwhelmed with emotions

And love for Zorko.



And then one day she told him:

'Zorko my love…I will be yours tonight

And I believe your words and your

Promise to love me forever'.

And they made love in the moonlight…

Under a starry night's cover

They became man and wife.

But as much as he loved her and

Cared for her

She was still afraid something might

Happen to their perfect love

And one day it did.


The world of darkness and of bad ghosts

Had sworn to take her away

As there must not be pure love on earth –

Never!


Zorko woke up and saw her

Taken away

While he was drugged by a dart

He could not help his young bride

And love.


A young and wonderful being

A sweet and fairy nymph

Out of the Fairyland of the Queen.

A just opening blossom

Not allowed to be opened up

To her full beauty

Not allowed to have a happy time

Not allowed to share her life and love

With her dearest Zorko.

He is suddenly utterly destroyed

In days of agony and pain

And he can find neither rest nor sleep

Since his beloved Zina is gone to the

Darkness of the Netherworld

To become a prisoner to the nasty

Creature:

The ugly Lord of the Flies and Flees.

Zorko stops shaken with emotion

Thinking of Zina and feeling his pain

Piercing his heart.

He cries:

'I am sorry my dear Queen

I'm so much in pain that I have to show it

To you here. Today.

TODAY!

But let me finish…

I will be just a moment'.




And soon he finds his voice again:

'I tried hard to find her' –

He closes his song –

'Everywhere I was searching but

In vain.

I have covered the tracks of

This world.

Until a good soul I found in this land

Told me to see you and ask for help

As you never have refused anybody

Especially in pains of the heart'.

He concludes and stands still for

A minute.

Then he falls to his knees and
He can't stop his tears running down
His cheeks and trickle into his shirt.
And the moaning crowds are hushed
Again by the Herald.

They stand still
Looking at the King and Queen.
Queen Nora of the Iceworld
Is moved.

Queen Nora is deeply moved by Zorko's ballad

Her head bent down a bit

She leaves her throne and

The somber king.

She comes down the steps to meet

The bard and her hands extend and

Help him to his feet again.




Zorko looks into the eyes of Queen Nora

He feels her human warmth and

A wave of radiant compassion.

Her teardrop falls to the floor

Turning into a precious stone.

She turns to face the king and she sees

He is moved as well.

Queen Nora addresses him –

Still holding the hands of the bard –

With a soft and articulated voice:

'King of Ice'. She starts.

'I have been deeply moved by

The plight

Of this unfortunate of bards.

I want you to extend your help

And use your powers as the mighty

And just king you are

And help this poor tormented soul

To find his precious love again.

Imagine it would be me! Would you

Not move a mountain to get me

Back again?'


The King of Ice feels the pain of his

Queen

Who feels out of sympathy for the

Unfortunate bard.

Her emotions are gripping his strong

Beating heart.

He composes himself with a gesture

Of his hands

And as his Queen returns to her throne

King Noro clears his throat.

The mountain trembles

As he commands his Herald to summon

The rock-faced Giants.


When the mountain has settled again

From its ramblings and trembles

The rock-faced Giants appear

With a mighty growl

And a roar like thunder.

These colossal pack of Rock-like men

Rise to the call of their commander

King of Ice.

Once the tremor of the Giant's stirrings

Has calmed down

Stillness enraptures the assembly

In King Noro's Hall.

The rock-faced Giants appear in King Noro's Hall

And in the hush the bard approaches

Thanking the king for his immediate

Attention

To his desperate human plea.

He knees in humility before the pair

Kissing the fine-boned hand of the

Queen

Delicate like porcelain extending

From the silken frills of her sleeve

Of her colourful body-shaping dress.

Stretching with her moves

Kissing the ridge of her hand and

Moving his head to meet her eyes.

Softening the pain in the poet's heart.


Her teardrop falling into the bard's hand

Which immediately closes on impact.

And when he opens it again

A diamond of lively sparkle and with

Great fire rests in the palm of his

Carefully-opened hand –

'Keep it for Zina' the Queen whispers

'It will bring her back! But give it to her

Only

Once she has passed the

Arches of the Netherworld'…

A slowly rising fog engulfs the hall

With Queen Nora's last words

The Royal Pair disappears

Before the poet's eyes.

Queen Nora's tear turns into a diamond in Zorko's palm

Zorko finds himself between

A mass of flowers

On the slopes of the giant mountain

Bedded on the carpet

Of its emerald green grass.

The colourful heads of a myriad of

Flowers perk towards the

Radiating and life-giving sun.

The morning's dew still glitters

In between their petals

Like the precious diamond

He had seen just before.

He still recalls the scene he has

Dreamt of:

Singing his song of love in front

Of the Queen of Ice and

Immediately his right hand

Searches his pocket.

And there his fingers feel the large

Polished facets of the huge

Pear-shaped stone

Which is the frozen tear

Of the Queen –

His secret to save

His beloved Zina from the

Clutches of Hate…

Guard at the entrance gate of the

Netherworld.


He dares not to take the diamond out

And have a good look at it

As someone might observe him

And spy upon his treasured crystal

Ready to steal it from his possession

Drowning all his chances of ever

Seeing and saving his love –

ZINA.


He stretched and wakes and he

Touches his face to assert he's

Alive himself

Like he would have escaped from

The magic of the underworld of

His dreams.

'Where is my beloved Zina?'
He cries out.
'How will I find her now?'
He laments.

Then he takes his lyre
And he starts to sing the song
He has composed and sung
For the Queen of Ice before
About his growing love
When he first met Zina.

But soon depression enfolds him
And tears will well in his eyes
As he passes the spot
Where they made love for the
First time.

And out of nowhere
Dark forces grabbed hold of
Zina suddenly.
She cried out
Her face in pain and fear

Distraught and agonized.

He lunged for her in vain

His arms suddenly paralyzed.

She was whipped off him

Her arms reaching toward him

In despair.




She turned into a white

Cloudy figure

Dissolving in front of his eyes.

Zina's Abduction

His heart began to bleed
His songs became his cries.
He has now to carry on living
To tell his sad and tragic tale.
And he began singing in such
Pain and agony
With such deep love and passion
His songs moved the heavens
And the earth.

The skies cried tears and
Planet earth began to change:
The tears became springs and the
Springs became brooks
The brooks became rivers and the
Rivers became torrents
Which flooded the entire earth
The mountains shook and sobbed.

The Giants rose from the depths
And cracked open the earth's crust
Lay bare the arches of the dark
And flame-flickering Netherworld.

Zorko thought it was the last of his

Thoughts

As the world shook to the rains

And storms and earthquakes moved

Below his frightened feet.


There was fire and ice

And flames rose so fiercely

They singed the tearful face of the bard

And with a huge bang

The tall mountain blew his top

Spew fire and ash and covered

The entire world.


Gone were the flowers

The green of the meadows

The deer was choked to death.

Zorko closed his eyes and held

His dwindling breath.

He thought his end is here

But he wanted to see his Zina so

Intensely

Nothing else would matter.


He held Queen Nora's diamond

Clasped in the palm of his hand

Thinking only about saving her

From behind the fateful arches

Of the dreading Netherworld

Which they had to finally pass

As Queen Nora had said.



His believe in the words of the

Queen was so strong and stand fast

That he could not be shaken or scared

The least bit

By the worlds own fiery and angry

Destruction.

Dark figures scuttled from behind
The smoke and sulphuric clouds
And burning acrid ash.
A dark grey shadow grabbed his free
Left hand and pulled him along
Into the distance and the sight of the
Netherworld
Into the caverns and the cliffs.
The winding road was filled with
Visions of death
And frightening witch-like images
Of ugliness
He shuddered from.

His right hand never softening
The grip on his life-saving tool
The tear-shaped diamond.

It was a hard and tiresome journey
With many ups and downs
On a rock-strewn path
Where nobody could pass.

Where many Sirens with their

Seductive dances would grab at

Him and lure him into their dim-lit

Dens of fleshly pleasures

Promising him eternal wellness

And a paradise of lust

No one ever could enjoy on the

Upperworld.


His lyre was strapped to his back

And seductive-sweet sounds did

Emanate

Strokes by skilled fingers

Of nymph-like hands and arms

Of a Queen

As if he had just seen the hands of

Queen Nora.


His mind beginning to play tricks

On him

He softened up

Could not see himself

To continue this trip any longer.

He saw many pretty women's faces

Around him

Stroking his face

Kissing his trembling lips and he

Felt aroused by their intimate touches.


As these scenes intensified

Feeling invaded and devoured and

Pulled into a pond f sexual pleasures

He could neither fight nor resist

Any longer

He collapsed and fainted.


The last image he saw was that

Of Queen Nora

Holding her tight and kissing

Her opening lips…

As he woke

He felt heavy like a stone

Fallen from the sky

A bandage around his head

The sound of bees buzzing in his

Hurting head.

Zorko's Seduction

There was a murmur and the sound

Of running waters nearby.

He got up and had a look through

Laced blue curtains

Onto a tumbling waterfall and a basin

Where young women took a bath.


But in the background he could see –

Maybe it was only a dream –

It was ZINA!

He cried out loud

But he had no voice.

He saw her bathing in the spray

Of the waterfall

In her nakedness

Innocent

But regal like a Queen.


But he could not be certain

If it was really her

As the picture changed every

Three seconds.

He fell onto a wide bed and he

Crawled below

Protective white sheets

Falling into a deep healing slumber.

Gentle hands woke him

A young woman was changing his

Bandages and she tended to his

Open wounds.

'You nearly died'. She indicated to him

With her hands and her face

As she was dumb.

Then she wrote on a pad:

'Suddenly blown off the road by a gust

Of wind

You fell into a deep ravine.

The local Amazons found you
Applied first aid and brought you
To their leader
Who commanded that you should be
Immediately taken to their physician's
Tent'.


The young nurse present and changing
His dressings
Indicates to him that he's healing
Rather well.
She assures him that he must rest more
So he'll be healed quite soon


'What's your name? `He asked.
She write on the pad: Stella.
'That's a pretty name.' .He said
She smiled and wrote him a friendly note
He answered with many more questions
And as Stella could not answer them all
She wrote on her pad:

'I will report all your requests together

With my progress report to my mistress –

Ama –

Ruler of the Netherworld Amazons'.

He nodded

Then he closed his eyes and relaxed

Soon he fell asleep.




Stella reappeared to help him dressing

Then she led him to the audience of Ama.

Zorko performs for Queen Ama of the Amazons

Stella arrived with Zorko at

Queen Ama's palace

The hall was already filled with a bevy

Of strong sinewy young women.

All hushed up as Queen Ama

Appeared

Accompanied by two dark leopards

And sat down on her throne.


She asked for the reason why Zorko

The bard would be attempting to

Venture into this dangerous valley.

And in return he would ask her permission

To sing for her.


A pretty maid brought him his lyre

And thus he began his song of love

That he had sung before to Queen Nora.

Slowly his song of a lost love touched

Al the women with feelings

They never knew they had before and

Even the worrier-women began to

Shed tears.

He moved the assembled tribes

The deer and the carnivorous beasts.


The Netherworld turned and cried and

The rivers swelled

Rising out of their beds.

Queen Ama had to stop the bard

Having heard his heart-gripping tale

Sadness beset her heart.

She ordered her personal guards

To guide him to the road he seeked

And to find his way to the Ruler of

The Netherworld.

Queen Ama gave him good advice and

She saw to it that he received his

Cleaned clothes

And his tear-shaped diamond.

'Before you leave dear bard'

She said

'Take a refreshing drink':

Then she bides him farewell and

Let him go to find his sweetheart

Zina

He so lovingly had described to her and

All the Amazons.


He does not recall the many places

He still encountered along his long

And stretching path

Meandering as in a labyrinth.


As Queen Ama had given him

A magical potion to drink

That steeled his heart and mind

Fending off the seducing Sirens

And held at bay the many traps

Through the 'Gardens of Desire'.

The longing to eat from poisoned fruit –

He had been warned –

Would turn everyone who just tasted it

Into a zombie –

A mindless coward.

Zorko gefangen im Labyrinth des Niemandslandes

Eventually

His feet burning with a fiery pain

Equaling his inner sorrows

He arrived at the Gates of Hell

The portal with the red and glowing

Fires

Lunging out behind steel bars

Forbidding anyone to enter

Unless so ordered by henchman Hate

The watchman of the gates

Whose red eyes stared at him.

Zorko took his lyre and intonated

His song of love.

And everybody stopped dead in

Their tracks.

The fires were dwindling and cooling

And the gate-man's mouth hung open.

Tyrant Hinod summoned Hate to get

The bard to him

As he wished to listen to his plead.

But as time passed

Zorko became weary

He sank to his knees and fell asleep.

Woken by the messenger sent from

The Ruler Hinod –

King of the Netherworld –

He had to appear to his court

At once!

Zorko the bard collected himself

Ordering his clothes to be brushed.

He freshened up

Washing his face in a nearby

Bubbling fountain.

Then he prepares for his important

Meeting with the fiendly lot.

He has now t stay at all reasons

Calm and collected and master his

Flaring emotions

To succeed with his plight.


Humming his tune

He prays to his Muse.

She'll help him at this last station

Of his quest and empower his feet

To carry him thru'.

Not let him falter now

When his task could lead

To good fruition.

But he knows that his will could be

Tested to the utmost endurance.

Doubt and fear could enter his mind

And pervade his body

Just at the most inopportune time.

He prays and mumbles and begs

And scrambles to sort his exited

And tested mind

To smother his soul and to clear

His heart of any doubts.


His Muse arrives silently on

Wings

Invisible to all bedeviled

The many more roach-like creatures

The wild and frightened animals with

Human faces

The human outcasts

And the scum of the earth.



The journey into the Netherworld

Is never ending.

Maybe that's why the word of its

Depiction had been chosen not only

For the deceased

And Zorko thought he would never

End up at the Gates of the dark faced

Hinod's

Glistening castle of coal ashlars.


There was a hurdle to gain access

With a goat-faced creature

Who seemed to guard the entrance

With an expressionless face

Indifferent with his black head and

White-yellowish body

Reacting not a cinch

Either to talk or to plea.

So bard Zorko began to sing.

He sang his song he could sing in

His dreams

About his quest finding Zina

His love

Taken from him brutally and violently

At their most tender moment.

He sings with such passion for his love

That even the animal-faced creatures

Crouch and seem moved.

And then suddenly

Tyrant Hinod's messenger arrives at

The Gate to the Black Palace.

He finds the singing bard and he

Raises his hand in a gesture

To follow him immediately.


Then the messenger will let him know

With gestured emphasis

That Tyrant Hinod had heard of his plead

But he had to be first convinced that

Zorko had indeed moved the land and

Earth with his haunting song of love.

Could he do the same with the entire

Netherworld?


The big dark hall is blistering in the heat of its

Fires

As it is progressively cold where the bard

Has to walk toward the lit-up ghost-like scene

Of the Black Palace.

Tyrant Hinod's palace from coal ashlars

The Ruler of Netherworld
Who will only visit for his audience a
And the assembly of ghosts and witches
And wretched mummified creatures
Gathered around the gloomy hall
Murmuring.

There is a sudden hush of the assembled
As the dark figure of Tyrant Hinod appears
Clothed in a purple coat
His face well hidden by a loose hood.
Just a gleam is seen at times to elope
From his dark and piercing eyes
Reflecting lightening glances from
The open fires.

His dark and somber appearance
Matches his metallic artificial voice
As he calls for the bard:
'You are Zorko the well-known bard?
Prove who you really are!'
His voice sends chills up the spine of
Everyone present

Including Zorko's
Who concentrates to collect himself.


Sliding his lyre from his back
He moves into his favourite position
The left foot set-up on a seat.
With one bent knee
He strikes his lyre with his bow.


The assembly is now dead still
As he intonates the first chords.
His lyrics form the song that captures
The surrounding dusky woods
The deer and the stones.
It moves the peasants and women
Artists and kings
As it had once moved Queen Nora
Who left her precious tear for him
To save Zina!
For her he would do his utmost
And sing his best ever.
His voice is soft and pleading and when
It cries as he sings about his quest

To find Zina his only love

Who was abducted by the

Shadow-ghosts

Of the Netherworld

So it seems.

ZINA.

She and her most gracious smile

Was all he really had.

He loved her so dearly that now he

Begs Tyrant Hinod to let her free and

Return with him to the Upperworld

Where she was content and

Bathed in his love

She prospered…

But now she must be waning like

A dying flower.


He is so unhappy as he sings about

The flowers and the deer and the

Happiness in nature

And the chances to have somebody

You are holding dear

As love conquers everything

And lets him endure hardship and
Pain.
And he would die in front of
Tyrant Hinod's flaming portals
If he could not get back Zina
His jewel
His light of his eyes.
He continues to praise her beauty
And her charm.
Her descriptions are deeply loving
And move the assembly of the
Dark and ugly creatures
The shadows of the night.

Even the crowd of disgusting witches
Seem to be hurting by his soul-catching
Love song.

It is all he requests:
Just to be with his beloved and no matter
Where he had to go or what he had to do
He would endure all
Just to get Zina back.

The ghosts who lined up in a file around

Him

Stood still.


Tyrant Hinod moved his arm and

All hushed up to a surprise freeze

As out of the pitch-black darkness

A white-hooded figure

Statuesque

Somewhat stooped

Passed in a floating-like movement

To the front where Zorko stared at her.

Recognizing her face and her dress

He cried out: 'ZINA!'


The tyrant silenced all with a mere

Command of his raised right hand

The poet sighed and his arms wanted

Immediately to take her.

His heart rejoiced in faster beats

He could not express his joy he had

Instantly felt

But finished his song with a cadenza

He had composed her at this very moment

Of great happiness.

Zina appears at the last chords of Zorko's love ballad

before Tyrant Hinod

Tyrant Hinod stood silent for a while
Then he pointed towards the arched gates
Of the Netherworld and announced
With his deep metallic voice
That Zorko's plead would only be fulfilled
If he'll keep his eyes strictly to the path
Not looking at her until he passes the
Arches of the Netherworld with her.


There were sounds like
Swooshing gusts of wind
The fires faded and the whole scene
Disappeared at an instant.
Animal-men and witches
Ghosts and creatures dissolved into the
White fog-like smoke and he
Could not see Zina
He wasn't allowed.
But he stuck to his promise and the path
Back
Toward the Arches of the Netherworld
All he cared about…

He supposed Zina followed him and he

Dared not even to raise the slightest sound

Or start humming a song

Or say a word.

He just talked in his heart and in his mind and

Kept going unperturbed by strange sounds.

Into his ears he plugged some cotton wool

And soon some real doubts set nagging the

Core of his heart.


Was it all just an illusion?

Was she really behind him?

As he couldn't hear a sound

Or the stepping of her feet

Yet he had talked to her silently all along

The long and winding path.

Well.

He had to fight his curiosity

Which now getting stronger and stronger

Beset his mind and thus pushed him forward.

He hurried his steps

Wishing that the arches would come closer

Faster. Faster! He shouted in his mind.

From his present distance he could see them
At times
Through some openings in the mist and the
Heavy drifting cloud.

He pinched himself not to fall asleep and
To hurry up
And get on with the task of reaching his goal
And claim Zina back.
He had to be steadfast whatever the price
He had to pay.

As more he wished the arches to arrive
As more he doubted he would reach them
By nightfall
And he began to panic.
Heavy drops of cold sweat covered his
Forehead.

He saw in front of him his Queen of Ice
And he watched himself been given her tear
Which formed into this tear-shaped diamond.
The precious stone with magical powers

To save Zina from the clutches of Tyrant Hinod
And the Netherland Shadow-Ghosts.
He saw the face of Queen Nora and her
Expression of genuine compassion and that
Gave him renewed hope and strength
To carry on regardless of his doubts.

Suddenly into his musings about his quest
To save Zina. His jewel…
The Arches of the Netherworld opened up
In front of him and with great eagerness
He passed through them
Using his last strength.
When he turned he saw Zina just under the
Arches
Slipping on a stone and not quite able
To pass entirely through the arches.
Zorko rushed back to take her into his arms
Pulling her through
He tried stopping her slipping back and
To save her from being lost forever.

Zina and Zorko below the Arches of Netherland

He passed his right hand into his pocket and

In one quick motion he held her and placed the

Threaded ties around Zina's head

To rest the tear-shaped diamond at her neck

Elated to have her saved.


But as he hugged her tightly

She started to fade. His heart stopped.

He cried out ZINA!

But slowly she turned into a white cloud

Uttering the words:

'I love you Zorko...forever'...


With that she completely disappeared

Like the morning's mist

In its dissolving dance.

The earth shook violently as she twirled away
And Zorko fell to his knees
Struck by a rock that fell from the top of the
Arches of the Netherworld.


Pandemonium erupted as the forces of the
Iceworld fought the Forces of the Netherworld
And Zorko was left for dead
The arches were destroyed
The entrance to the Netherworld was blocked
And disappeared.


Thunder and lightning crashed down to the
Troubled world and rivers swelled and
Angry torrents washed away all in their path.


Destruction ruled once again.
Zorko was nowhere to be seen and yet
There was somebody who was present:
A shepherd

Having seen a light above the glacier of the

Huge darkened mountain:

A beam with two white figures floating

Hand in hand

To the sounds of the most haunting music

One could hear out of the

Colossal mountain's caves

Just after a torrid thunderstorm.

ZINA AND ZORKO UNITED

The shepherd found a diamond

Pear-shaped and with unusual fire

And magnificent colours

When the sun was hitting its many polished

Facets.


He praised himself in good luck

Fascinated by the diamond's lively sparkle

But did not see a bear moving toward him.

When the huge bear growled

It was too late for the shepherd t run

Away.

But then the bear killed the unfortunate

Guy.



Someone else found the big precious stone

And called it 'Tear of the Queen'.

As he found it nearby the Iceworld's palace

Of the King of Ice

And he was well aware of the story of

Zorko and his quest to find his beloved

Zina

Who abandoned her precious gift

As she preferred Zorko above all other

Possessions.

That was her wish: To be united with her

Lovers forever

In the land of eternal ice.

ICELAND.


Today one may visit the museum of the

National Arts and Crafts and see the

'Tear of the Queen'.

But there must be so many

Because most countries with a Queen

Seem to have one in their scepter.


But whenever one enters the caves to

The eternal ice in the Giant Mountain

You may hear Zorko playing.

But one has to be in love to hear his

Song of love he composed for Zina

And locals tell you

You can hear its echo around the

Feast of Easter

Reverberating through the caverns

Of the Giant mountain.


Fin

A note to ‚King of Ice‘

The history for the components that provided the basis for the birth of the poetic legend 'King of Ice', reaches back for a long period of time.

When my Mom-in-law visited us in South Africa, where we lived for many years, my wife and I took her on a tour of the country.

We travelled through the Karoo to Cape Town. From here we decided to drive along the 'Garden Route', and to stop at the world famous 'Kango Caves'. She remembered her father, a natural history teacher, and she told us about his discovery of a prehistorical cave in the Loser Mountain, in the 'Dead Mountains' in the province of Styria, in Austria.

His discovery of prehistorical cave bear heads and bones was spectacular, and he spent many weekends to salvage his findings, tirelessly, often day and night. He crawled alone in the cavernous mountain, its soft limestone structures hollowed out by ravines from melted ice. Preparing his findings in his house, he reconstructed a complete cave bear, whose giant skeleton could be viewed at the local museum in Bad-Aussee, Steiermark.

While my mother-in-law and I were visiting the Kango Caves, her story had not only fascinated me, but stirred my fantasy as we walked between stalactites and stalagmites.

Later, on one of our visits to Austria, my wife took me to the 'Dachstein Rieseneishöhlen' – the gigantic ice caverns of the Dachstein

Mountains – where the awesome icicled landscape fascinated us with the luminescence of the icicle stalactite and stalagmite curtains.

The colourful display through lighting placed another layer of unforgettable pictures, of this ice-world's atmosphere, into my mind's collection of photographic sceneries.

Many years later, on a trip to the Canary Islands, the semi-tropical island of Gran Canaria placed yet another layer of images on the existing ones in my mind. It was all about the creation of this island through a volcanic eruption rising dramatically out of the sea, forming Mt. Teide.

The process of creation has through a long journey assembled a rich source of images, which were brewing in the melting pot of my artistic being. Finally, many years later, as I came across a series of photographs I had taken in the 'Rieseneishöhlen', I began to draw scenes to the ballad I had composed.

I had written the text in a poetic form about my experiences in caves. When the inspiration for the story came to me, I wrote it in one go. A most happy moment for any poet, and an accessible work for everybody.

I wish all my readers, young, mature, and the elderly folk, happy and enjoyable reading.


Z J Galos.

Further books from the author:

(Also available in the German language)


*The Mill below Owl Castle –*

*(Zols sentimental education)*


*Zora's Mistake –*

*(The potential of a hidden error)*


Published soon in both languages.

ZJG.